W9-BJK-649

VOLLEYBALL

BROWN

PHYSICAL EDUCATION ACTIVITIES SERIES

Consulting Editor:
AILEENE LOCKHART
University of Southern California
Los Angeles, California

Evaluation Materials Editor:
JANE A. MOTT
Smith College
Northampton, Massachusetts

PHYSICAL EDUCATION
ACTIVITIES SERIES

VOLLEYBALL

GLEN H. EGSTROM

University of California, Los Angeles

FRANCES SCHAAFSMA

*California State College
at Long Beach*

WM. C. BROWN COMPANY PUBLISHERS
DUBUQUE, IOWA

GV 1017 .V6 E3

Manufactured by WM. C. BROWN CO., INC., Dubuque, Iowa
Printed in U. S. A.

Preface

Volleyball has long been one of the most popular sports in our society. Its development, however, has suffered at the hands of well-meaning but uninformed proponents who have been unable to teach the refinements of play which are fundamental to high caliber volleyball. The name itself has become a misnomer since the object of the game is not volleying at all. The object is to drive the ball down onto your opponent's side of the net with such force or accuracy that it is impossible to return. Unfortunately, the beginning player is too often exposed to the game in the former sense over a sagging net. The satisfactions which can be derived from keen play are denied and no one is the wiser.

It is the purpose of this book to present volleyball as a sport requiring all of the speed, strength, endurance and coordination found in any demanding team effort. The skills, many of which are demonstrated in the sequences by Miss Sharon Peterson, U.S. Olympic Volleyball Team, are *fundamental* to well-executed play and should not be considered too advanced for the average player.

The strategy and play patterns are representative of the many variations which can be taken advantage of by special player talents. The book, in its essence, is a guide to *better* play and will, we hope, stimulate new players to acquire skills which will raise the general level of play in our educational as well as recreational institutions.

Self-evaluation questions are distributed throughout the text. These afford the reader typical examples of the kinds of understanding and levels of skill that he should be acquiring as he progresses toward mastery of volleyball. The player should not only answer the printed questions but should pose additional ones as a self-check on learning. Since the order in which the content of the text is read and the teaching progression of the instructor are matters of individual decision, the evaluative materials are not positioned according to the presentation of given topics. In some instances the student may find that he cannot respond fully and accurately to a question until he has read more extensively or has gained more playing experience. From time to time he should return to such troublesome questions until he is sure of the answers or has developed the skills called for, as the case may be.

Contents

1

What Volleyball Is Like

Volleyball has achieved great popularity in all countries where it has been introduced. This is due in part to the lack of highly specialized equipment and facilities and a reasonably simple set of rules. Volleyball is also a very adaptable game, modifiable for various numbers of players, different sexes and ages. It is popular as a men's, women's and coeducational activity. It is usually introduced, with modified rules, at the grammar school level. The more skillful aspects of the game are gradually included so the official rules are often well understood by junior high school groups.

Recently volleyball was recognized as the most popular participant sport in the United States. This estimate of player participation undoubtedly includes the game as it is played with various modifications since only a relatively small number of people play volleyball with strict observance of the official rules. Because the game can be and is played by so many, with great differences in amount of skill, there is general lack of appreciation for correct ball handling during the early learning stages. This weakness is gradually being overcome with clinics, training films and additional publicity which stresses "power" volleyball.

The official rules call for six players on a team and the object of the game is to cause the ball to strike the floor on the opponent's court or to cause an opponent to engage in faulty play. A net, suspended across a 60′ x 30′ court, provides the playing area. Each team is arranged with three players across the front of the court near the net and three players behind them across the back court.

The game starts with the players facing the net and the right rear player of the team which won the toss stepping out of bounds behind the court. This area behind the end lines is the serving area. The server strikes the ball sharply causing it to fly over the net to the defensive team. The receiving team must then field the serve and return it over the net using no more than three hits to do so. This pattern of three hits is basic to the game. Ideally, the first hit is a pass to the center forward player, called the setter. The setter then boosts the ball parallel to the net so that one of the front flanking players can drive the ball into the opponent's court, preferably with such force that it cannot be returned before it hits the floor. If the receiving team is successful in returning the ball to the serving team, then the servers have three hits in which to put the ball back over the net. This exchanging is called a rally and continues until a team commits a fault or fails to return the ball over the net.

When a team wins the service all of its players rotate one position clockwise in order to bring a new server to the right rear corner. A team must hold its rotation order until the ball is served, at which time rapid rearrangements enable players to move into advantageous positions. It is sometimes confusing that during this rearranging a back court player may move to the front court as a setter or blocker. This is legal, but the back court player may not lift his feet from the floor to spike the ball unless he moves into the back court. This ruling prevents one or two players from dominating the game. In coeducational play at least one of the three hits must be made by a girl for the same reason.

Points are scored only by the serving team and one point is awarded for each rally which is successful for the servers. If the receivers win the rally they then become the servers and are eligible to score points. A game is completed when a team scores 15 points. A tie at 14-14, however, calls for additional play until one team succeeds in gaining a two point advantage. A match usually consists of a two out of three game series.

The sport of volleyball is well suited to today's living since it can be played and enjoyed by people of all ages. It also provides the opportunity to acquire a group of skills which can be used for many years in an almost injury free environment. At the same time it provides a highly competitive, action filled exercise pattern for large muscle groups. The level of competition and activity is regulated by the skill level of the players but it can be appropriately strenuous at all levels.

Most of us recognize that we feel better if we have regular, more or less vigorous activity in which we can find relief from the tensions of work. Exercise contributes to the maintenance of muscle tone, helps control weight and provides much needed exercise for the heart muscle. For many years community Y.M.C.A. programs have sponsored "noontimers" volleyball for businessmen. Here an individual has opportunity to relax in friendly, good-natured play with peers who are also seeking an outlet for their need for activity. During recent years the development of more adequate community recreation facilities has led to increasing numbers of evening volleyball periods for adults. These programs are usually co-recreational and so provide the married couple a chance to engage in a sport together. School programs have also recognized the growth of facilities and interest and are making an effort to prepare their students with sufficient skills to enable them to feel a sense of accomplishment while engaging in play.

At the beach the mobility of the game is well demonstrated. Two uprights, a net, a ball and 180' of rope (or lines scratched in the sand) provide a court which can be set up in 10 minutes. Many beaches, in fact, have courts or at least uprights in place throughout the year in order to meet the growing demands for recreational volleyball.

The following chapters will provide you with insight into the nature and requirements of this sport which brings pleasure and healthful exercise to so many people in the country.

2

Skills Essential
for Everyone

The game of volleyball, when properly played, requires that the participants make specific adaptations to the artificial environment and value system of the game. This requirement is often overlooked by beginners who rarely identify the problems whose solutions lead to increased efficiency and effectiveness in play.

The dimensions of the courts (30′ x 60′) and the barrier (7′4¼″ for women and 8′ for men) indicate that short, quick movements and jumping are critical skills which are required in order to adapt to the physical limitations of the court. The light, well inflated ball necessitates the development of ball handling skills which result in a high degree of control both in direction and magnitude.

Moving quickly on the court depends upon adequate strength and endurance coupled with alertness. The strength and endurance requirements are quite specific and should be met through drills or game situations that involve the body in the exact movement roles appropriate to the game and with ever increasing work demands. If there are adequate levels of strength and endurance, the readiness of the individual becomes the critical element. Too often players stand erect, hands at their sides, waiting for the ball. When it comes they must raise their hands and arms, bend at the knees and then start to move. Logically the time taken to prepare to move is wasted, since the preparation could have been incorporated into the waiting stance. The "ready" position for volleyball thus is one in which the knees are slightly bent, hands are carried near shoulder height, elbows are up and away from the body and attention is focused on the ball. Caution: when moving to field a ball, take your steps *before* you begin to bend and reach—this will result in better control of the movement and you will be able to handle "low" balls much easier.

Jumping in volleyball is usually performed near the net. This means that the jumping style must be adapted to keep the player from touching the net. The tendency to jump forward results in fouls. It is important, therefore, to learn that you must move to the place where you wish to jump and then transfer essentially all of your momentum so that it goes up parallel to the net. Beginning players who jump and fly through the air become a hazard to teammates and a help to opponents.

Ball handling skills are probably the most critical skills to be developed since the circumstances for their application change very rapidly during play. The following skills are presented with the knowledge that extensions and modifications will be dictated by the demands of each play situation.

THE SERVE

The serve is extremely important because it is the only way to make points. It is necessary to do more than just get the ball over the net. Each player on the team should be able to place a serve accurately anywhere in the opponent's court. Any time you can put the opponents on the defensive with your serve, you are that much closer to winning the game.

The first consideration when serving is to be aware of body position. The server must remain in the service area and may not step on a boundary line of that area. Avoiding service faults is of prime importance and the best remedy for hitting a ball into the net, ceiling or out-of-bounds is purposeful practice. Thinking through the entire serve, taking a good deep

Figure 1—The Overhand Serve

If the hands contact the ball on a pass in the manner shown in the diagram, in which direction will the ball rebound? What adjustment must be made to cause the ball to take the proper trajectory?

Evaluation Questions

PASSING THE BALL

breath, exhaling half of it and relaxing before executing the movement take just a few seconds and should result in a good serve accurately placed.

The Overhand Serve—This serve is used by the majority of leading players because it can be placed accurately and if delivered correctly will "float" or wobble, putting the opponent on the defensive because he will have to make a quick adjustment to receive the ball. It often causes the receiver to make either an off-center or illegal pass.

The right-handed server stands facing the net with the left foot slightly forward. The ball is tossed with both hands, to prevent it from spinning, to a height 2′ to 3′ above the head and about 1½′ forward of the shoulder. The right arm is brought back and cocked and then as the elbow leads the way, the arm is extended so that the player is reaching with a fairly straight arm as the ball is contacted solidly with the heel of the hand. If the ball is tossed too far forward the hand contacts it above the center line of the ball and it probably will not clear the net. On the other hand if the ball is tossed too close to the head it will be punched to the ceiling or perhaps hit out of bounds. It is important to hit behind and slightly below the center of the mass of the ball to avoid knocking it out of bounds to either sideline. To make the ball float and drop it is necessary to keep it from spinning during delivery. Contacting the ball in line with the upper arrow in Figure 2 will cause a downward flight—a net serve. Contacting the ball in line with the lower arrow will usually result in a serve which skims the net and is difficult to field.

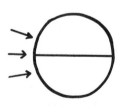

Figure 2—Flight of the Serve

Diagram A:
PASSING THE BALL

The Underhand Serve—This is a good consistent method for getting the ball over the net; however, it does not have the effect of the overhand serve because it is generally not difficult for the defense to receive and pass. It is easy to learn to place the underhand serve but seldom does it put your opponents on the defensive.

Figure 3—The Underhand Serve

7

From a position halfway between the rear court line and the net, take several quick strides forward to a spot two feet from the net. Can you jump into the air as high as possible from a two foot take-off and land in the same spot?

Evaluation Questions

Stand facing the net, knees bent, with the left foot forward and the left arm extended across the front of the body. The ball rests on the palm of the left hand. The right arm is swung straight back, then forward to strike the ball with the heel of the hand or the flat fist (palm forward). The head should be bent slightly forward as this helps to keep the ball lower so it will skim the net. As the ball is struck you step forward with your right foot as you follow through with the swing of your right arm. Again it is important to contact the ball solidly and directly at the point which will result in a proper trajectory.

The Roundhouse—This is a difficult serve to master and is not considered a safe one because it is hard to learn to use it consistently. The roundhouse can be delivered with great force but the top spin makes it follow a very straight course so it is not too difficult to judge and receive it. By just getting into position for receiving the ball, the opponent can gain impetus for his pass from the force of your serve.

The server stands with his left side to the net and tosses the ball about 3' into the air above and slightly behind his right shoulder. The knees are bent and the feet are spread. The right arm is swung back in an arc and the heel of the hand contacts the ball with great force as the wrist is snapped. The fingers are held rigid in a cupped position so they touch the top of the ball, imparting spin. The right arm continues around in the follow-through.

THE PASS

For the novice volleyball player receiving the serve and passing it is one of the most difficult skills to master. The ball is often missed completely, an illegal hit is made, or the ball is sent out of bounds or perhaps sprained fingers may occur. The cardinal rule for receiving the serve is to *get in position under the ball.* The head is back, elbows out, hands up, knees bent and one foot a little forward. The fingers are slightly cupped so all fingers and thumbs contact the ball at the same time. The ball never touches the palms. Lay the wrists back and make the palms face the ceiling. Index fingers and thumbs should form a triangle that you can look through to receive the ball. The thumbs point to each other from about 11″ apart. The wrists should be bent back and as the ball is contacted the wrists and knees straighten. A clean pass cannot be made easily with the elbows close to the sides. Recall the "ready" position with elbows up and away from the body.

The ball is most easily passed in the direction the player is facing and since the player receiving the serve always wishes to pass the ball to the front center of the net, position is of prime concern. The pass should arch high in the air, hang and drop without spin to the set man

Figure 4—The Overhead Pass

Is this body position correct for the forearm bounce pass? Why or why not?

Evaluation Questions

BODY POSITION FOR
FOREARM BOUNCE PASS

(center front player). He can then set the ball to the player on either side of him for a good "kill." The pass is such a very important part of the game that many hours of practice need be devoted to it.

Figure 5—Forearm Bounce

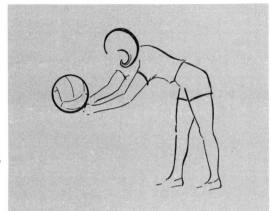

Diagram B:

BODY POSITION FOR
FOREARM BOUNCE PASS

Often it is necessary to go completely into a squatting position in order to get under the ball for the pass. There are emergency methods for receiving a low ball or recovering a loose ball but the better players always use the pass when possible even if it means falling to their knees or sitting on the floor.

*The Forearm Bounce Pass—"Bump"—*The forearm bounce pass is used for recovering a loose ball, a hard driven serve received below the waist or a spike in cases where it is not possible to get under the ball for the safe, conventional overhead pass. It is a skill to be developed by all players but should never be used when the overhead pass is possible. This pass is aptly named since the ball merely bounces off the flat surface of the clasped hands, wrists or forearms and there is not much follow-through. If the arms are swung into the ball it will probably hit the ceiling or go out of bounds. The purpose of this skill is to bounce the ball into the air as a recovery shot so that a teammate can get under it to make the set-up.

To get into position for the forearm bounce pass, the player quickly clasps his hands together and rotates his elbows inwardly with forearms parallel to the floor. The knees are bent slightly in order to assume a crouching position with the left foot slightly forward. The ball is contacted directly with the flat extended surface of the forearms as the knees straighten in a smooth motion to bounce the ball upward. The bump can be used to recover a ball on either side of the player by extending the arms to the side and presenting a flat surface to the ball.

*The "Dig" or One-Hand Bounce Pass—*The "dig" is a recovery shot used for a ball that is received low and off to the side of a player. It is

Have a partner throw the ball into the net. Using the forearm bounce pass, can you play the ball over the net? Can you do this on 3 out of 5 trials? on 5 consecutive trials?

Evaluation Questions

similar to the two hand bounce pass. The arm is extended with the hand cupped slightly and the wrist held rigid but flexed just a little to direct the ball in an upward bounce rather than out or down. The weight is carried on the balls of the feet to allow rapid change of position and the

Figure 6—"Dig" or One-hand Bounce Pass

knees are bent to the crouching position. As the ball is contacted squarely with the slight curve of the wrist and heel of the hand, the knees are straightened for the follow-through. The ball is hit with just enough force to lift it into the air for the set. It is most important to keep your eye on the ball in order to contact it squarely so it will not go out of bounds on either side.

Evaluation Questions

Place a line three feet long at a height of five feet on a clear wall surface. Standing three feet from the wall, can you volley 10 consecutive forearm bounce passes above the line? 15? 20?

The one-hand bounce pass can also be used to recover a ball that is going to drop behind the player. If it is not possible to back up quickly enough to use the overhead pass, the arm can be extended behind the head to punch the ball up and forward with an easy wrist action. This shot should be used carefully. The player should always be alert and ready to move rapidly in any direction in order to be able to use the overhead pass whenever possible.

The Net Recovery—If the ball is hit into the net on the first or second contact it is possible to keep it in play if it can be bounced into the air again. The forearm bounce pass or the dig is used for this recovery shot. When it is performed correctly it looks easy and smooth. The most important consideration in this shot is watching where the ball strikes the net. A ball landing near the top of the net will drop almost straight down. If it hits the center of the net it will rebound out a foot or two before dropping. A ball that contacts near the bottom of the net will most often be held by the net momentarily before rolling out and down.

The player watches the ball and with experience and practice can determine where to position himself for its recovery. He turns his side to the net and crouches in order to contact the ball as close to the floor as possible. If it is to be the second hit the player should try to bounce the ball up and back to avoid hitting it back into the net. This also gives his teammate a better opportunity to spike or place the ball on the third hit. If it is to be the third contact with the ball, the player attempts to

How can X₁ and X₂, spikers, improve their positions to await a set from 0? Why is an approach taken on a spike?

Evaluation Questions

WAITING POSITION
FOR SPIKE

hit it up and over the net. This particular shot is difficult to achieve but can be done with practice.

THE SET-UP

Most teams are divided into four spikers and two set-up players. As soon as the ball is in play the front set places himself between the two spikers unless he is already there from the rotation process. Changing his position from either side to the center after the ball is in play is called "switching." The set-ups should be the two best ball handlers on the team. It is necessary to be well coordinated and very agile to become a good setter.

Assuming that the first player to contact the ball makes a perfect pass to the setter it is easy for him to make a good set-up for one of the two spikers. He stands with one side to the net, knees bent, back arched and head up. The ball is contacted as in the overhead pass, with the setter looking through the triangular window formed by his thumbs and index fingers. By taking a step back as the ball is contacted he can set up the spiker he faces. If he takes a step forward he can easily set up the player behind him. The setter should delay taking this step until the last second in order to keep the opponent blockers unaware of who will be receiving the ball. The setter places the ball between 1½' and 2' from the net and at least 5' above the net. As in the pass, the ball should arch, hang and then drop directly in the position desired. Through the use of signals the setter can let his spikers know to whom he is giving the ball and where they will receive it. By setting up the ball at either corner of the net it is easier to spread out the blockers on the opponent's team.

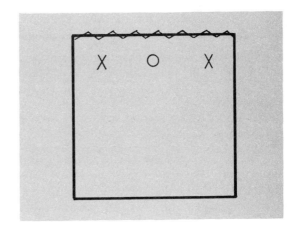

Diagram C:

WAITING POSITION
FOR SPIKE

Even though the setter does not receive a perfect pass from the back line and it is necessary for him to move under the ball he should be able

Figure 7—The Set

to set up his spikers for the kill. The second ball always goes to the front set unless he calls for help from another player.

The setter should know his spikers and know where they like the ball placed. With purposeful practice, teamwork will evolve that permits the players to use numerous variations of the set and thus improve their effectiveness.

THE SPIKE

The spike constitutes one of the most difficult to coordinate acts found in any sport. The player must be able to run, jump high, time a moving ball, hit it solidly, and at the same time try to place it in a certain spot. It is a spectacular skill to observe and even more spectacular to perform.

The spike is varied by almost every player to his individual preference; however, a great deal of study has been made of this skill and there are certain actions which must be performed to accomplish a hard, fast drive on the ball.

The two-foot take-off is the accepted starting procedure. The spiker adjusts his position at the start in order to run in a straight line toward the net and ball rather than approaching from an angle. The run is made from 10′ to 12′ back and varies among players from a long stride to short steps or a glide. The crouching position is assumed in order to give more impetus to the jump. The jump is made approximately 3′ behind the ball so it is above the head and about a foot in front of the spiking shoulder. The player does not come up under the ball. As he jumps both arms are flung up and the upper trunk twisted sideways to the net so the spiking right arm is back. The left arm is carried higher for balance. As the left arm is driven down, the shoulders become parallel to the net. The elbow leads as the spiking arm whips forward and it acts as a pivot to prevent the arm from hitting the net. The arm straightens as the wrist snaps forward to drive the hand into the ball. With enough height to the jump, the ball can be hit with the heel of the hand as the hand and fingers are snapped forward. The ball is directed over the net and down into the court.

The player must be prepared for his spiked ball to be blocked, in which case it would drive right back down at him. He must also be balanced to prevent falling into the net or over the center line. The defense for these problems is handled in the follow-through. The player lands with knees bent and elbows close to the body for balance and with hands ready for a quick dig on a blocked ball.

Figure 8—The Spike

Even if the ball is set up too far back from the net for the conventional spike, it still can be attacked in much the same manner. The ball is contacted slightly behind the head with the heel of the hand or cupped hand. The fingers are held rigid and the hand slapped around the top of the ball thus imparting top spin. The top spin causes the ball to drop in a sharp arc.

Common faults in spiking are hitting the ball out of bounds or into the net. These faults can be remedied with the development of proper timing, a sufficiently high jump, and proper position of the hand as contact is made with the ball. Timing is critical since hitting the ball during its ascent will tend to result in hitting under the center of mass of the ball. This will result in a trajectory which will carry the ball out of bounds. Hitting the ball too late during its descent can result in a net or missed ball as a result of hitting on top of the ball. Proper timing will permit the ball to be struck as it appears to "hang" during the period when the ball is changing direction from ascent to descent or during the early stages of dropping while the ball is still well above the net. The ball should be struck with the heel of the hand, fingers carrying over the upper part of the ball, with the ball 1'-2' in front of the shoulder of the spiking arm. Striking at the ball with the fist will often result in a wild hit since the timing becomes even more critical. Striking with the fingers will usually result in an illegally handled ball.

A common fault in jumping for the spike is leaving the ground too soon. One must learn to time the jump so that you reach your maximum height at a time when the ball is just beginning its drop. Jumping too early will result in the predicament where the ball continues to move away from the spiker and stays just out of reach during ascent as well as descent.

3

Better Players
Master These Techniques

Volleyball has been identified as the most popular participant sport in America. It should be recognized, however, that this statement includes all levels of play and varieties of conditions. Enjoyment is possible with rather limited skills but as the players improve their skills the satisfaction derived from the game increases many-fold. As the skill level increases attention to the "fine points" of the game becomes a necessity. The following material is presented with the thought that while beginners may have some difficulty in executing advanced movement skills effectively, it is necessary to understand them in order to make them ultimately a part of your game.

Probably the most critical skill for you to learn is "court sense." Court sense is the ability to be in the right place at the right time by reacting to your opponent's game so that you are always in good position for either offensive or defensive play. Better players continually adjust their positions during play even when they do not appear to be directly involved in the action. They are always ready for the unexpected. This court sense is augmented by the ability to "dig" the ball while moving rapidly.

The development of court sense is speeded up if you get into the habit of determining how you can position yourself on each play in order to be most effective. Think about the elements of the game. Ask yourself, "Was I in the best possible position during the rally?" The following example should help you to understand this point. Your opponents have just fielded the ball and passed to the setter. He in turn is making a high set which permits your team to put up a three-man block.

19

If a three man block were to be used by this team, which man would join X_1 and X_2? Why?

Evaluation Questions

THREE MAN BLOCK

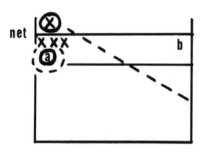

Figure 9—Spiking Against a Block

This situation, which puts three men in the air to block, leaves two particularly vulnerable areas to be covered. Area "a" is vulnerable to a "dink" unless another defensive player moves up to cover this area and "b" is the spiker's most clear hitting angle. Unless you or your teammates can move into these areas *before* the spiker makes his decision, it is not likely that you can recover the shot. Covering the block in this fashion must be done automatically each time the block is used.

Another advanced skill is "digging" with one hand. Most beginners after a little experience begin to field the ball while moving. The next step is to learn to move so that you can get the forearm and heel of the hand between the ball and the ground so the ball will rebound into the air on your side of the net. To "dig" effectively you must learn to play the ball low. This gives you more time to place your hand in the proper position for a good pass. The sequence could be described as follows. Determine where the ball is being driven. Move quickly in that direction, taking care not to bend at the waist until you are within reaching distance of the ball. When you have moved to the ball, reach for it holding the heel of your hand and the flat inner surface of the wrist so that they present as flat a surface as possible to the ball. Remember any knob or

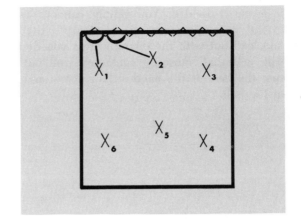

Diagram D:

THREE MAN BLOCK

irregular surface will cause a deviation in the rebounding characteristic of the ball; therefore cup the wrist rather than extending it.

Spiking the ball is, for most beginners, a very difficult skill to master because it depends upon several critical factors. First a good set is necessary. Only very advanced players learn to hit the "bad" ball while almost anyone can learn to hit a good set. The would-be spiker must learn to move away from the net so that he can hit the ball out in front of his body. Most beginners get caught at the net with the set coming down over their head. When this happens the tendency is to reach over the head and try to hit the ball. Rarely is the ball driven down; usually it is bumped high and slowly goes to the opponent where

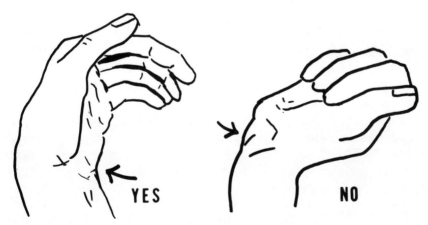

Figure 10—Proper Hand Position

21

it is easily fielded. You simply cannot develop a powerful hit if you extend your arm over your head to hit the ball. You must cock the arm and lead out with the elbow just as you do when you throw a ball hard. The volleyball must be contacted well out in front of the shoulder so that the heel of the hand strikes above and behind the center of gravity of the ball.

4

Progress
Can Be Speeded Up

A technique for improving individual play that has been used quite effectively involves learning to play with progressively fewer players on a side.

The teams play with the customary six on a side until the rules and most fundamentals of the game are understood. Then the teams are reduced to five on a side for two or three periods of practice, then four, three and finally two. If this progression is timed appropriately, the players become accustomed to moving quickly to the ball and making their passes and sets more effective. After moving through the progression (four to six weeks), the players are reorganized to six on a side. The resultant play is usually dramatically improved since players have learned about the importance of readiness to move and court position. This form of practice also incorporates the improvement of conditioning in a game situation.

Effective serve placement can be developed if the server imagines a six-part division of the court and practices dropping his serve in each one of the six divisions. The skill developed in this kind of practice will enable the server to follow weaker fielders from position to position and force them to move to their weak side to field the ball. Accuracy in serving can also be improved if the server develops a consistent pattern for handling the ball during the preparation for service. This includes details such as the placement of the valve, since the valve causes a slight imbalance which can affect the flight of the ball.

A self-improvement technique which has been helpful in bettering the skills of many new players is called mental practice. This form of

Can you cause five consecutive serves to land within eighteen inches of the right side line? of the left side line?

Evaluation Questions
FOOTWORK

practice requires that the individual focus his concentration on patterns of movement he has learned; he introspectively rehearses the skill to be improved. For example, in improving the spike one could introspectively rehearse timing the moving ball with the jump to proper height and the body movements involved in hitting and following through. It has been suggested in various experimental studies that such introspective rehearsal can result in marked improvements in skill. It is a practice widely used by high level performers and can be applied when the individual is away from the game. This focus of concentration can also be helpful in developing the court sense, or the ability to know where and when to move, since you can analyze imagined game situations involving a variety of problems.

The development of specific skills and fundamental maneuvers can best be accomplished by practicing them purposefully in drills which

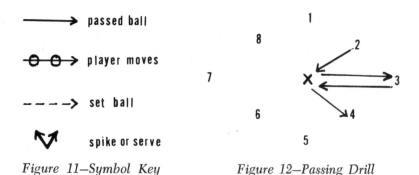

Figure 11—Symbol Key	Figure 12—Passing Drill

are game-like. Following are examples of how fundamentals can be incorporated into patterns which will be similar to game situations. The symbol key is as follows:

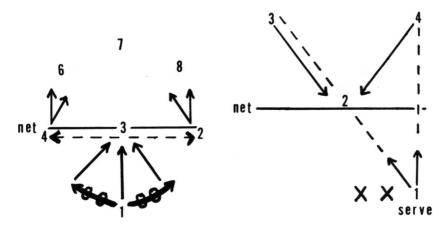

Figure 13—Multiple Skill Drill   Figure 14—Game Drill Situation

1. The formation in Figure 12 is used to practice passing and setting to various distances and locations.
   Center player passes to each player in the formation. At the conclusion of a full circuit center then moves to #2 while #1 moves to the center; all other players move one position clockwise.

2. The formation in Figure 13 can be used to practice pass, set, spike and blocking or digging.
   The pass from #1 is received by #3 who sets to either #2 or #4 for a spike. The defense can field the ball or attempt a two- or three-man block. All players rotate after two or three turns in the same position. Note: bad passes to the setter and bad sets to the spiker should be played as if a point were at stake.

3. The formation in Figure 14 uses service, service receiving and passing. It is important to remember that the drills should involve the application of skill in ways very similar or identical to the game situation and that the same effort should be put into practice as into a game.

Place a 1' x 1' marker two feet from the net and halfway between the sidelines. From the right back position, can you pass the ball to a height of 10 to 15 feet so that it lands on the marker? from the center back position? from the left back position? Can you do five successive hits from each position?

Evaluation Questions

4. A simple drill for developing ability to recover balls from the net is shown in Figure 15.

Player A passes the ball into the net at various heights and distances from player B who must then move into position to field it and bump it into the air, preferably as a set since the ball in the net usually occurs on a bad pass and only one hit will remain after the recovery.

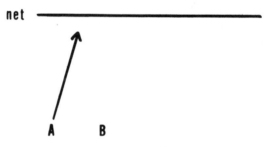

Figure 15—Net Recovery Drill

Patterns of Play

Team play is *essential* in volleyball. The effectiveness of any team is proportionate to the coordination of the abilities and responsibilities of its members. Outstanding spiking does not occur without precision setting. The setter's ability to place the ball for the spiker depends largely upon the ability of the team's members to control the ball on the first volley as it comes from the opponents' court. Each player must do his best in order to enhance the team's play.

Each game situation places new and different demands upon each player at each position on the court. Successful teamwork requires that a player know all the team patterns which have been established, think quickly and anticipate situations before they arise, and make maximum effort to carry out his responsibilities.

OFFENSIVE PATTERNS

Basic Pass Pattern—The spike is the key offensive weapon in volleyball. To insure opportunities for the spike, a general pass pattern is used. As the ball comes over the net from the opponents' court, whether on a serve or a rally return, an attempt should be made to *pass* the ball to the center front player, who is known as the *setter*. The setter then *sets* the ball to either the left front or right front player for the *spike*. The *pass-set-spike* pattern is the basis of volleyball offense.

The right and left front positions are considered to be the spikers' positions, because the distances to the farthest boundaries of the opponents' court are generally longer from these positions than from the

Evaluation Questions

TEAM PLAY IN SPIKING

> X_1 is spiking against a well-skilled team of opponents. What are the positions taken by this 3-3 team called? Why are they necessary?

center front. This affords the spiker a choice of angles for the spike with the assurance of the greatest possibility of keeping the ball within the court boundaries. Figure 17 illustrates the angles for the spike.

The primary responsibility of the setter is to take the pass from the service receiver and set it into a position where the spiker can attack the ball. The setter should attempt to face either sideline squarely while setting for the spike. This positioning assists the player to achieve accurate ball-handling. The setter should also feel obligated to get to the ball for

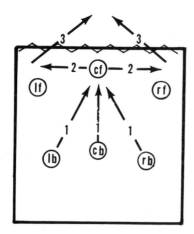

Figure 16—Pass, Set, Spike Pattern

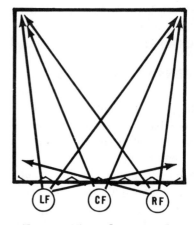

Figure 17—Spiking Angles

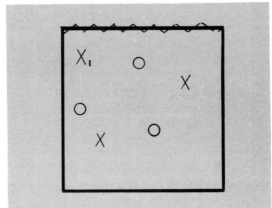

Diagram E:

TEAM PLAY IN SPIKING

the set if it has been placed anywhere near the center front position on the pass. If, after the pass, the ball is in a better position to be played by a teammate of the setter, this teammate should quickly and verbally call the setter away from the play in order to avoid confusion and possible collision. If the pass should go to one of the spikers, he has the choice of spiking the ball or executing a cross-court set to the opposite spiker.

Set placement depends upon the desires of the spiker and the game situation. Spikers prefer that the ball be placed anywhere from three to eight feet above the top of the net, and usually very close to the net. The height of the set varies with the game strategy and the individual timing of the spiker. Variation in height of the set will cause the opponents more difficulty in executing the spike defense. A good setter should become thoroughly aware of the desires and capabilities of each team-mate in regard to the set.

In women's play shorter players who cannot execute the acutely angled spike can make a spike-type hit which places a good deal of top spin on the ball and which is effective if it can be placed in the deep corners of the opponents' court. Hitting behind and below the center of gravity of the ball with a sharp upward pressure causes the desired top spin.

Team Alignment—At beginning levels of play the basic team align-ment is such that each player upon reaching the center front position be-comes the setter, while left and right front players are considered to be spikers, regardless of their special capabilities. This is called the 6-6 arrangement. As experience with the games increases, it will be discerned

29

that some players are more effective as spikers than others. If all six members of a team are good spikers the 6-6 alignment should be continued. This situation rarely occurs, however. It is more likely that a team will have a maximum of three or four spikers. If this is the case, the capabilities of the spikers can be used to full advantage. The value of the remaining members of the team cannot be overlooked. The work of setters in accurately placing the ball for the spikers and in court coverage on defense is invaluable to any team.

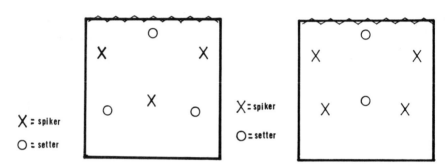

X = spiker
O = setter

X = spiker
O = setter

Figure 18—3-3 Player Arrangement   *Figure 19—4-2 Player Arrangement*

If three spikers compose the team's offense, the 3-3 alignment is used. This is also used in coeducational play, with the women assuming the setter positions and the men the spiking positions. Where four spikers are available, the 4-2 alignment will be effective.

Due to the differences in positioning of setters and spikers occurring through rotation, both the 3-3 and 4-2 arrangements require adjustments to obtain the advantage for the spikers. The rules of the United States Volleyball Association permit players to switch positions on the court after the ball is contacted by the server. These rules are used for all men's play, coeducational play, and some women's play. Most women's games, especially those played in schools and colleges, are governed by the rules published by the Division for Girls and Women's Sports, in which the persistent swiching of players is prohibited. Refer to Chapter 7 for details in reference to this rule.

When switching is permitted, spikers and setters can assume more advantageous positions on alternate rotations. Figures 20 and 21 illustrate the exchange of positioning for the 3-3 and the 4-2 alignments, respectively. Note that the setter always positions himself near the net to await

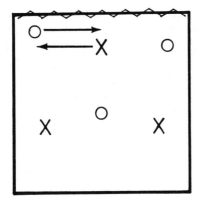

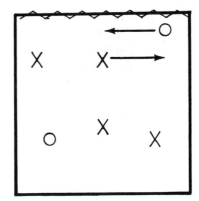

Figure 20—3-3 Setter, Spiker Switch

Figure 21—4-2 Setter, Spiker Switch

the exchange, whereas the spiker is several steps from the net. This puts each in correct relationship to the net after the exchange and eliminates the possibility of confusion in movement.

Whether or not the switch in the 3-3 alignment is made is determined by the team. If the nonswitching procedure is used the spiker can be positioned toward either side of the court in order to cause the opponents' defense more difficulty. The pass pattern shown in Figure 22 shows the spiker offset to the left side of the court. This same pattern may be reversed for the right side of the court. In addition, if the pass goes to the right or left setter, the set can be made directly above the setter's position with the spiker moving in to execute the hit. Of course these variations require that teammates be coordinated in their movements and that the spiker be agile and quick moving.

If the switch is used, players must be sure to hold position until the ball is contacted on the serve. The serving team exchange usually is not difficult. The receiving team, however, must concentrate on a quick switch without interfering with a strong reception of the serve. Refer to the later section on receiving the service for a diagram suggesting procedures.

Covering the Spike—The well-executed spike will be "put away" to win a rally at beginning levels of play. As the opponents gain experience in the use of the spike-blocking defense, the offensive team must be alert to react to possible return plays. If the block is successful, the ball may rebound to the spiker's side of the net. Very often the blocked

31

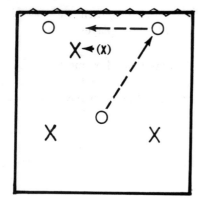

Figure 22—Spiker Off-set to Left

Figure 23—Covering the Spike

ball will drop back over the spiker to the area on the court just behind him. It it necessary for the spiker's teammates to be ready to cover this possibility and to try to reset for another spike to regain the offensive.

The diagram, Figure 23, indicates the movement of the spiker's teammates when the ball is set to the left front player. All players should be alert, in a ready position with the hands carried at shoulder level. The left-back player moves in quickly to cover the short block. The center back swings to the left and along with the right back covers the deeper back-court area. The center front and right front players move back and slightly to the left to cover the angle possibilities in their respective areas.

In this coverage plan, it is important that each player move quickly and work to regain control of play so that the spike attack can be re-assembled.

DEFENSIVE PATTERNS

Receiving the Serve—The server who can place the serve or who can create deceptive floating or spinning action of the ball is on the offensive. This makes the receiving of the service a defensive maneuver. The serve must be handled and controlled before the receiving team can assume the offensive.

Careful observation by experienced teams and coaches has indicated that the majority of serves in most volleyball games fall into the middle third of the receiving team's court. For good coverage, then, the receiving team should flood this center court area with each player aware of the area for which he has responsibility.

Figure 24 shows the recommended alignment for most men's or women's play. The center of the half-circle arrangement is positioned toward the server. Since the server can put the ball into play from anywhere behind his own rear court line, adjustments may be necessary if the server varies the serving position.

The two front line players who have dropped back to cover the sideline areas should be alert to move forward to handle short serves to the sides of the court. The center front player is prepared to set for the spiker if the serve comes short to the center area. The backline players must be prepared to cover the area a step or two ahead of them, cover behind the sideline players, and move to cover the entire backcourt area. For good team coordination, players should become accustomed to calling verbally for the ball, saying for example "mine," "yours," or "take it."

Each member of the receiving team should take a stance which will permit him to move quickly in any direction. It is suggested that all players take a balanced stance with one foot slightly ahead of the other, and with the knees flexed. The hands should be carried at shoulder height. This is called the "ready position."

The variation for receiving service, as shown in Figure 25, is recommended in switching offenses where the left or right front player is to

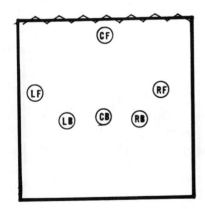

Figure 24—Receiving the Serve

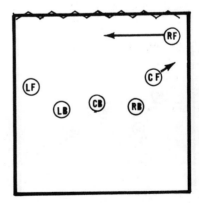

Figure 25—Receiving the Serve
(switch variation)

When a switch is desired, what error in receiving the serve is being made in this 4-2 arrangement?

Evaluation Questions

POSITIONS FOR

A SWITCH

move into the center court as the setter after the serve is contacted. The potential setter must place himself near the sideline so that the center front player can take a position in the receiving line-up without being positioned illegally in relationship with his teammates.

The two illustrations, Figures 26 and 27, give the receiving positions for coeducational play. In mixed volleyball it usually is preferred that a man field the serve for the pass, which should go to a woman, who in turn sets to the spiker, a male member of the team. This alignment calls upon the men to anticipate a wide range of lateral movement in order to cover the court adequately. The women are placed in position for

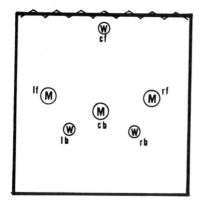

Figure 26—Receiving the Serve
(co-ed, two women back)

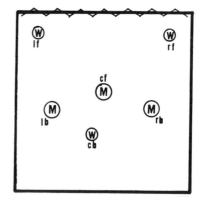

Figure 27—Receiving the Serve
(co-ed, one woman back)

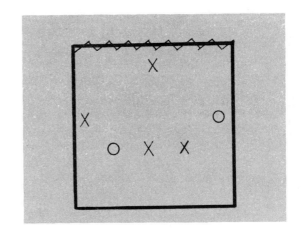

Diagram F:
POSITIONS FOR
A SWITCH

setting, or handling the second hit, should the receiver be unable to play the ball directly to the setter.

According to the United States Volleyball Association rules, front and back line players may not overlap positions with one another until after the service. In addition, players within either the front or the back lines may not overlap positions until the ball is contacted by the server. In play, according to the Division for Girls and Women's Sports rules,[1] each player must be in her respective sixth of the court at the time of service. Players should be alert to avoid being stationed illegally while receiving service as prescribed by the rules used to govern play. Violation of the rules results in a point being scored for the serving team.

Spike Defense—Blocking the spike, which is equivalent to placing a barricade of hands in front of the spiker, is essential to good defense. This becomes increasingly more evident as opponents develop power and control in executing the spike play. Without the block to divert the attention and intention of the spiker, the possibilities of fielding the well-hit spike are very limited.

The number of players used to block the spike varies with the degree of proficiency of the spiker. A two-player block is used in women's play, as well as in coeducational play, while the three-player block is in common use in men's play, but it appears that the two-player block will soon replace it.

Regardless of the number of blockers employed, the mechanics of the blocking teamwork remain the same. As the ball comes to the opponents' setter, all possible blockers move directly forward to within twelve to fifteen inches from the net, with their vision focused on the ball. This

35

With this team alignment (M — men, W — women) which players form a block at the right front? Which player covers the long angle past the block? Who covers for the drop volley?

Evaluation Questions

DEFENSIVE PLAY

movement is illustrated in Figures 28 and 29. As the setter places the ball for the spiker, the blocker directly opposite the spiker assumes the placement for the block jump. Meanwhile the remaining blockers slide sidewards toward the initial blocker until arm or shoulder contact is made with the teammates. The jump for the block is coordinated so that there is no more than three to four inches between all of the blocking hands. The end hands are turned in toward the net to contain the spike. The player at the net who is away from the direction of the set falls away from the net when he sees the set placed in order to assist in covering the remaining area of the court.

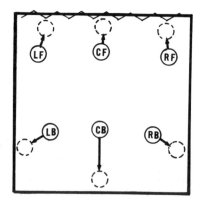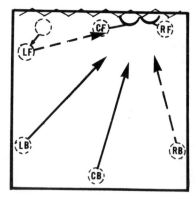

Figure 28—Blocking Pattern (two man)

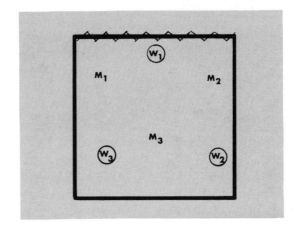

Diagram G:
DEFENSIVE PLAY

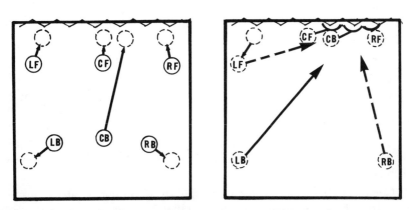

Figure 29—Blocking Pattern (three man)

All players not participating in the block are responsible for covering the remainder of the court. As the set is made to the spiker, all nonblocking defensive players are deployed to extreme spots on the court to cover all angles of potential returns past or over the block. As the spiker goes into the air the player directly behind the block and the player nearest the net begin creeping forward toward the play. These two players must be prepared to pick up all soft drop volleys, or dinks, over and to the sides of the block, should the spiker choose not to spike. The other defensive player(s) hesitate until the spiker's arm is cocked for the hit. At that moment a fast break is made directly toward the play at the angle of the anticipated spike. With this movement the spike past, through, or

37

over the block may be fielded, or the ball which bounces into the air off the blocker's hands can be played with good control. This type of defense puts the team "on the move" and facilitates active and aggressive court coverage.

The two-player block is shown in Figure 28. Note that the dotted line refers to the slow moving players, and the solid line indicates the movement of the hard driving play toward the spike.

The formation of the three-player block is shown in Figure 29. Note that the third player comes to the net from the back line. It is easier for this player to move forward than for the third front line player to move sidewards under good control.

The illustrations given are those used against a spike from the opponents' left front play. To defend against spikes from the right front, the formation of the defense simply is reversed. If opponents vary from the standard offensive pattern, adaptations can be made using the basic concepts of team organization for spike defense discussed in the foregoing pages.

Judgment must be developed to know when and when not to form the block. Usually a block is not necessary if the setter misplaces the set. If the spiker will be off balance or if the set is excessively distant from the net, the block should be called off, and blockers should drop back from the net to assist in court coverage of the return. In the situations described, the average spiker usually will be unable to execute a strong, sharply angled spike, and the defense will have better court coverage by not blocking.

Coeducational play presents a slightly different strategy problem. Most often the men attempt to absorb all the power aspects of the game. The blocking therefore is done by the men, usually a two-player block, utilizing the third man to field the back court area for balls past, through, or over the block. Figures 30 and 31 suggest blocking procedures with the two different alignments encountered in the 3-3 positioning of coeducational play.

The Spirit of Team Play—If a team is to be successful it is necessary for all members to play the game to the limits of their abilities. The thrill of a good performance can be experienced again and again by the player who is mentally alert, and who will make every possible effort to carry out his assignments. An even greater thrill is in store for the player who will seek, through his own play, to enhance the performance of his teammate. Complete confidence in, and respect for one's teammates is the basis of real team play.

VOLLEYBALL AND THE FUTURE

The foregoing patterns of offense and defense are those considered to be fundamental to the game of volleyball as it is played in the United States today. The mastery of skills and strategies by players around the world yearly brings a new look to the game. From these fundamental patterns the creative thinker and strategist may devise new and interesting variations and departures which will add to the fascination which is so much a part of this exciting and thrilling sport.

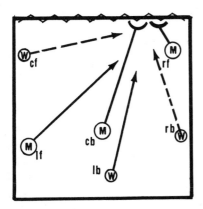

Figure 30—Co-ed Two Man Block

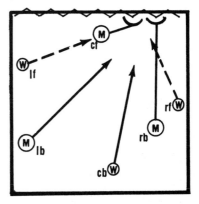

Figure 31—Co-ed Two Man Block (alternate)

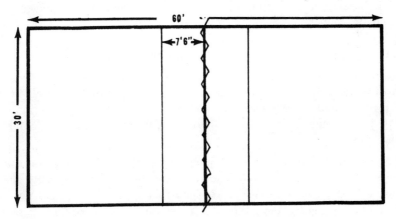

Figure 32—Court Diagram

Language and Lore
of Volleyball

Volleyball originated in the United States in 1895 and has gained such popularity through the world that it was included by the Japanese, as host country, in their 17 selections for the 1964 Olympic Games for both men and women. There have been considerable improvements in the two pieces of equipment necessary to play the game since it was first devised by William C. Morgan, a student at Springfield College and later director of the Holyoke, Massachusetts, YMCA. Prior to Morgan's graduation, he devised an idea for a new game which he called minonette. Borrowing skills from tennis, handball and baseball, he erected a tennis net at a height of 6'6" across the center of the gym. A rubber bladder from a basketball was used for the ball. Any number of players were allowed on each team and the object of the game was to hit or bat the ball back and forth over the net. The game was played in nine innings and each server had three outs before his team lost the ball.

Morgan took his game to his first job and introduced it to businessmen as a relaxing game, somewhat less strenuous than basketball. It was well received and in 1898 was reviewed, renamed "volleyball" and published in the proceedings of the Springfield College YMCA Sports Conference of that year.

Morgan also wrote the A. G. Spaulding & Bros. Company the specifications for a more suitable ball and there has been no appreciable change made in its design in the 70 years since that time. The official net used at this time is lighter than the tennis net and affords resiliency so that players can pick up a rebounding ball.

The YMCA instructors learned the game at Springfield but as they took it to the various YMCA's around the country they made modifications and revisions in the rules to accommodate special needs.

The original rules recorded in 1896 called for the game to be played in nine innings on a 25' x 50' court. The top of the net was supposed to be 6'6" off the ground and the ball 27" in circumference with a weight of nine to twelve ounces. The server stood with one foot on the back line and had two chances to bat the ball over the net. He was allowed assistance on his serve but no dribbling. A point could be scored only by the server. A net ball, after the first serve, or a line ball, was considered "out." Players could not touch the net or hold the ball and could dribble within only four feet of the net. A ball rebounding from any object outside the court was still in play.

In 1900 the YMCA brought volleyball to Canada, Central and South America and to the Orient, where it was not very popular for many years but is now widely played. In 1900 the YMCA Physical Directors Society adopted a new set of rules which eliminated the dribbling, first bounce and the innings. The game was now played to 21 points over a 7-foot net. The line ball was declared good and the ball could no longer be played off objects outside of the court.

Volleyball was introduced in Cuba in 1905, at the first annual convention of the Playgrounds of America Association (now the National Recreation Association) in 1907 and in Puerto Rico in 1909.

In 1912 the YMCA appointed a special committee to recommend rule changes. This committee moved the net higher, to 7'6", and made it 3 feet wide. The court was enlarged to 35' x 60' and a rule was devised for rotation of players. The serve could no longer touch the net and the two-game match was originated.

One rule which has remained virtually the same and which signifies the spirit of volleyball was recorded during the first YMCA Open Invitational Tournament held at Germantown, Pennsylvania, in 1912—the players called their own fouls. This annual tournament was held for the next ten years.

The education profession recommended volleyball for all school and recreation programs in 1915 because its value as a team sport was realized, together with baseball, basketball and football. During the ten years that followed numerous rule changes were made. In 1917 the net was placed at eight feet and a game played to 15 points. The next year the six-man team was established. In 1921 the center line was put under the net and

How should the player attempting a net recovery alter his foot position?

Evaluation Questions

POSITION FOR
NET RECOVERY

in 1922 the rule for hitting the ball only three times on each side was introduced. The court was made 30′ x 60′ in 1923 and it was decided that a team had to make two points in succession to win if the score reached 14-all. This rule was revised in 1925 to read that a team needed two points more than the other team in order to win if the score reached 14-all.

The evolution of the game to its present form was completed by 1925 and included the 8-foot net, six-man team, the marking of a center line, three hits on a side, 30′ x 60′ court and the 15-point game, with ties at 14-14 being settled by a two-point margin.

Volleyball is generally supported and controlled through the direction of the United States Volleyball Association, which includes representation from other interested groups such as the YMCA, Armed Forces, National Collegiate Athletic Association (NCAA), Amateur Athletic Union (AAU), American Association for Health, Physical Education and Recreation (AAHPER), etc. The volleyball association was organized in 1928 by Dr. George Fisher who is known as the "Father of Volleyball" and who from 1917 until his retirement in 1953 was the editor of the first Volleyball Guide published by the American Sports Publishing Co. of New York. The NCAA and the YMCA worked jointly with Dr. Fisher in editing the rules for the first Volleyball Guide which today serves to describe volleyball activities in all parts of the United States and which has been edited and published annually by the USVBA since the formation of that organization. A system for standardizing tournaments, qualifying officials and selecting representative teams has also been developed by the USVBA.

Volleyball as an international sport owes much of its prominence to the U.S. Armed Forces, which, as early as 1919, had distributed over

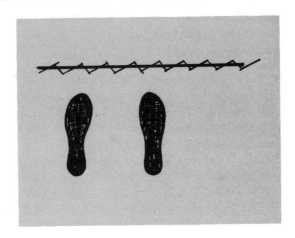

Diagram H:

POSITION FOR
NET RECOVERY

16,000 volleyballs to the American Expeditionary Force and its allies (USVBA Guide, 1965). During World War II our servicemen carried the game all over the world. It is now played in more than 60 countries by more than 50 million people. It is the leading sport in 25 countries and ranks third internationally. The sport is especially popular in Japan and Europe. The first world's championship was held in Moscow's Dynamo Stadium in 1952. Julien Lenoir[2], then Secretary-Treasurer of the International Volleyball Federation which was formed in 1947, noted that 99 per cent of the 60,000 spectators understood the rules and appreciated the performance of the players in those games. The Federation, located in Paris, governs international rules and the annual world's volleyball championship. It is ironic that an American volleyball team has never won a world championship even though volleyball in this country has celebrated its seventieth anniversary. This curious fact is due, in part, to the development of a difference in rules and interpretation in European volleyball that has led to an advanced style of play which has been difficult for Americans to accept.

The enthusiasts in any sports area develop a jargon or specialized language to cover the specific skills and their applications in the games. Volleyball is no different and, although the jargon changes from one part of the country to another, the terms which are covered here are common to most places where volleyball is played extensively.

As the game opens, the six players on each team are arranged in rotation order with three front court and three back court players. Since this rotation order must be observed at the time of service, it is common to see a *switch* occur. This switch allows a temporary rearrangement of

43

What is the term used to denote the movement to one? to two?

Evaluation Questions

POSITION CHANGES

players after the serve and permits a spiker and setter in the front court to exchange positions so that the setter is between two spikers. From this position the setter can set the ball to either side. A *back-set* can be used to set the ball up to the spiker behind the setter. This advanced skill is somewhat difficult to execute in a *clean* manner. This term refers to a ball's being distinctly hit, that is, it may not be carried, handled or juggled while it is in play. Examples of plays which are not clean are a *double,* or double hit, wherein the ball is played with one hand or touches another part of the body before it is contacted by the other hand, or a *throw* in which the player has a delayed contact with the ball. This is also referred to as *sticky* ball handling. The development of a pair of clean hands takes a great deal of practice. Concern about consistent rulings on clean plays has led to the virtual elimination of plays in which the open hand or hands are used to field the ball below the waist. Even though many beginners find it more simple to use open hands in an underhand motion to field low balls, it is wise to avoid this habit. While it is easier at first, it becomes a distinct source of trouble as your play improves. It is much better to learn to *bump* or *dig* the ball as described in the skills section of this booklet. The dig, as a skill, was probably developed on the beaches in Southern California where it is common to see *two-man* volleyball played on sand courts. This extremely fast and highly skilled play results in many occasions where the players dive head-long along the sand to field the ball, thus digging it and keeping it in play.

During play it is not uncommon to hear words with special meanings. Frequently when a ball is spiked one of the blockers will call *one.* This

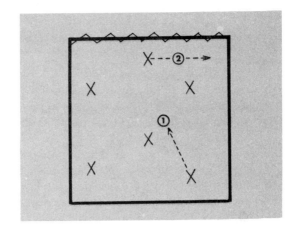

Diagram I:

POSITION CHANGES

means that the ball was hit or touched by one or more of the blockers and that only two hits remain to return the ball over the net. Occasionally a spiker, seeing that he is confronted by a good block, will *dink* the ball. The dink is a light tap that drops the ball just over and behind the block. It is for this reason that one player is usually assigned to *cover* the block, meaning that he must be prepared to move into the area behind the block to field the "dink."

If a spiker runs too far under a set he may change his hitting style to a *roundhouse*. In this maneuver the spiker swings a straight arm in an arc until he contacts the ball, thus imparting a topspin to the ball with a good deal of force. It is effective as change of pace and will sometimes be used as a serving technique as well.

A player who touches the net will call *net*, thus indicating that play should stop as result of his foul. It is expected that the individual call this foul on himself in the best tradition of the game even though this is not required in the rules. This tradition has been a part of the game since the early 1900's when volleyball tournaments became better regulated and formalized. This custom of calling fouls on one's self has been a key factor in improving the level of play in beach volleyball where it is usually impractical to have an official. Players develop the habit of calling "throws" as well as net violations. The players who does not call his own fouls soon finds it difficult to play with the better players. *Jungle ball*, a loose form of volleyball in which mishandled balls are accepted, is not acceptable to players who are knowledgeable about the game.

As the game progresses and the score reaches 14, it is common to call *point*. This indicates that one point is needed to win. It will also be used when approaching the two-point advantage needed to overcome a tie after 13-13.

Contributions to playing techniques have been developed internationally. The *spike*, for example, is reputed to have been introduced by a little-known team in a tournament in Manila.[3] This "backwoods" team had the habit of passing the ball high in the air so that a large, rangy bushman could run in and hit the ball. The opposing teams had no defense for this maneuver and, since it did not violate any existing rules, it has developed into a highly-skilled art, the practice of which makes the game an exciting spectator as well as participant sport. Dr. Charles McCloy, a researcher from the University of Iowa, published material stating that a volleyball spike travels an average of 62 m.p.h. with exceptional shots attaining speeds of 110 m.p.h.[4] Recent material, in an attempt to corroborate these findings, has indicated that the maximum speeds are, however, considerably less than 110 m.p.h. Yet the point remains that spikes travelling nearly 100 feet per second require a high degree of defensive skill and quick action if they are to be recovered.

In tournament play it is remarkable that a spike rarely hits the floor without contact by a defensive player. Some players, in fact, become so skilled that they field the ball with their feet when they cannot move rapidly enough to get their hands on it.

A recent innovation which had its beginnings in Europe has been largely responsible for the success of the Japanese women's Olympic team. They have developed great skill at diving to field the ball and then tumbling back to their feet to be ready for the next play. This team, which had not been defeated in three years at the time of this writing, practices strenuously for two hours prior to a match and spends a great deal of time perfecting these tumbling techniques.

Many innovations have also been developed as a result of the refinements in the game as it is played on the beaches, particularly in Southern California. The court dimensions are regulation but only two players are available to cover this space. In recent years, two-man women's play has improved to the point where the play is nearly as fast and aggressive as the game played by the males. This type of play has, in fact, been instrumental in the revision of women's rules until they have become very similar to the men's. Within the women ranks an identical set of playing rules has been developed for most levels of competition and a strong central organization functions within the United States Volleyball Association.

One of the areas of great weakness in volleyball in the United States, however, centers in the school framework. Even though the game is widely played and widely taught, the techniques for higher levels of play have frequently been neglected. This is usually due to a lack of understanding on the part of the teacher who finds the game easy to control and teach to the point where everyone enjoys it. The progress in skill development at this point is dependent upon stressing "clean" ball handling and adherence to the rules concerning play at the net. "Throwing" the ball can be perfected to the point where a player who *might* become a good, "clean" player is reluctant to discard the skills which make him effective in a loosely played game. This lack of attention to progressive development in play unfortunately results in relatively little improvement during the junior and senior high school days.

7

Rules of the Game

Rules governing play in volleyball have evolved throughout the years, since the origin of the game. As different groups played in various settings, rules were advanced to suit the individual situation.

Though an effort has been made to standardize play throughout the United States, there are several differing sets of rules in use, depending upon the affiliations of the group sponsoring the competition. In addition, the rules governing international competition differ in many respects from those which are in effect in amateur volleyball in the United States.

Currently most volleyball competition in the United States is played under the rules established by one of two rule-making bodies. The United States Volleyball Association, affiliated with the Amateur Athletic Union, has established rules which are in use in virtually all men's competition, whether on interscholastic, intercollegiate, or amateur level. All amateur women's competition, and most coeducational and recreational league play is also played under the USVBA rules. The second rule-making body, the Division for Girls and Women's Sports of the American Association for Health, Physical Education and Recreation, publishes a set of rules used for most interscholastic and intercollegiate competition for women and girls.

In reality there is little difference in the actual playing of the games under the two sets of rules. The following sections are designed to give a summary of the USVBA rules, with exceptions noted where these occur according to DGWS rules, or are necesasry for coeducational adaptation.

THE COURT, NET AND BALL

The volleyball *court* playing surface measures thirty by sixty feet. It is bounded by lines two inches in width, and is divided into two identical square court areas by a two inch *center line*. There should be at least a twenty-foot *space above the court* which is free of obstructions. There should also be a six-foot area beyond the rear of each court area known as the *service area*. If this amount of space is not available, the serving area should extend into the court the distance necessary to afford the server a six-foot area.

An additional line is placed seven and one-half feet from each side of the center line and parallel to it. This line is known as the *"spiking line"* and governs the spiking area for back line players. (Exception: DGWS—contains no reference to the seven and one-half foot line, although back line players are prohibited from spiking at the net.)

A *net*, measuring three feet by thirty-two feet, is tautly stretched from all four corners across the court over the center line. The height of the top of the net is eight feet from the floor for men's play and coeducational competition, and seven feet and four and one-quarter inches for women's play.

The *volleyball* is twenty-seven inches in circumference and weighs approximately ten ounces. The outer casing, which should be laceless, is made of either leather or rubber. The inflation of the ball should follow the manufacturer's instructions.

TEAMS, PLAYERS, POSITIONS AND SUBSTITUTES

A volleyball *team* consists of six players positioned into a front line and a back line of three players each. At the time the ball is contacted on the service, the front line players must be totally in front of back-line players, and all of the players within either line must be positioned so that their feet in no way overlap. After the service all players may move to play or cover any area of the court, with the stipulation that a back line player executing a spike must leave the floor from behind the seven and one-half foot line. (Exception: DGWS—(1) all players must be in their respective sixth of the court at service, assuming the court is divided into thirds in width, and into a front and back area; (2) after the service, players may cover any court area but may not persistently interchange positions; and (3) a back line player may not spike at the net, but no limiting distance from the net is given. Coeducational—Men and women must take alternate positions in the serving order.)

Are these men and women (M and W) in legal positions for receiving a serve?

Evaluation Questions
RECEIVING A SERVE

Players must follow the *serving order* established with their positions at the start of the game. After the loss of service by the opponents, the serving team *rotates* one position in a clockwise direction.

Substitutions may be made upon request of and recognition by the official anytime the ball is dead. A player may enter the game three times, provided he enters each time at the same position relative to his teammates which he occupied at previous entries. (Exception: DGWS— (1) a fifteen second time-out is taken to complete substitutions; and (2) only two entries per game are permitted.)

PLAYING THE GAME

A *match* consists of three games. The team winning two out of three games is declared the winner. The *game* is played until eight minutes of actual playing time is concluded, or when one team has scored fifteen points, whichever occurs first. In either case the winning team must lead by two points before play is concluded. *Actual playing time* begins at the time the ball is put into play at each service, and the time clock is stopped each time the ball is dead after each play.

A *toss of the coin* determines which team will serve first and which court each team will occupy, the choice being given to the winner of the toss and the loser receiving the alternate choice. Teams *change courts* after each game and at eight points or four minutes into the third game. The team not serving first in the first game serves first in the second game, and so on. (Exception: DGWS—the team losing the previous game will begin serving in the next game.)

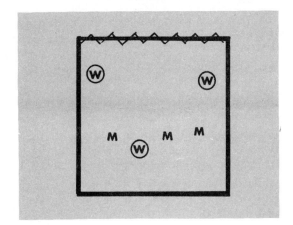

RECEIVING A SERVE

Diagram J:

Three minutes is taken between games for rest and reorganization. Each team is permitted to call two team time-outs per game, the length of the time-out being one minute.

The game is started with a *service* by the right back player on the serving team. This player must be outside the court and within the service area until the ball is contacted on the serve. The ball may be hit or batted with the hand, fist, or arm, and is directed over the net into the opponents' court. The server continues until his team loses the service or until the game is completed. When one team loses the service its opponents will serve after having rotated one position clockwise. During service it is illegal for a team to screen the server's action from the opponents' view in any way. It is also illegal for a team to serve out of order. If the error is discovered during the service, all points scored during that service are deducted and the service is terminated. If, however, the error is not discovered until after the opponents have served after the illegal order, no penalty is assessed but positions must be corrected. (Exception: DGWS—the screen for service is legal, provided each player is in her own sixth of the court.)

After the service the ball must be *clearly hit* when it is volleyed by any player. It may be contacted with any part of the body as long as a player does not play the ball twice in succession, and provided that the part of the ball contacted is on that player's side of the net. If the ball contacts two parts of the body at the same time, this is considered to be one play. Simultaneous contact of the ball by teammates or by two opponents constitutes one play, and either player may play the ball again. In addition, if a player participating in a multiple block contacts the

51

ball, he may play it again. Each team may play the ball only three times before it crosses the net to the opponents' court. A player may go outside the court to play the ball as long as he does not cross the imaginary extension of the center line. (Exception: DGWS—(1) the ball may be played only by the hands and forearms; and (2) the blocker's play on the ball constitutes one play and that player may not again touch the ball until it has been played by another person. Coeducational—if the ball is played by more than one player before sending it into the opponents' court, one play must be made by a woman.)

When *playing at the net,* a player may not touch the net or its cable while the ball is in play. Neither may he reach over the net to play the ball or to follow through any otherwise legal play. The ball may be played off the net. It is legal to touch the center line but illegal to touch beyond it into the opponents' court. It is also legal for a player to reach under the net to play a ball which is in play on his court, but it is illegal to reach under the net and interfere with opponents' activity. (Exception: DGWS—a player may follow through over the net providing any contact with the ball is made on her own side of the net.)

The *completion of a play* is considered to have occurred when all participating players have reached equilibrium and are under full control. This means that if in concluding a play at the net a player should fall into the net or onto the opponents' court, the foul is called even though the ball may have been dead for several seconds.

CONDUCT

It is considered to be unsportsmanlike to shout or stamp the feet while an opponent is in the act of playing the ball. Persistent comments to the official regarding decisions or making derogatory remarks to or about either officials or opponents also are considered to be gross misconduct and unsportsmanlike.

FOULS AND ERRORS

A *foul* is an infraction of the rules. An *error* is a failure to play the ball properly. The *penalty* for both fouls and errors is a point scored for the opponents or side-out (the loss of service). (Exception: DGWS—no distinction is made between fouls and errors.)

Fouls are called whenever (1) the server is out of the service area before the ball is contacted; (2) any player is illegally positioned on the service; (3) screening of the service is used; (4) a back line player leaves the court for a spike closer than seven and one-half feet to the net; (5) a player serves out of order; (6) a substitute returns to the game in a position other than his original one, in relation to teammates; (7) a server unnecessarily delays putting the ball into play; (8) a player touches the net, reaches over the net, crosses the center line, or interferes with opponents under the net, while the ball is in play; (9) a player enters the game more than three times or otherwise substitutes illegally; (10) a player conducts himself in an unsportsmanlike manner; (11) a player delays the game in any unnecessary manner; (12) a team calls more than two time-outs per game. (Exception: DGWS—(1) screening the serve is legal; and (2) a player may enter a game only two times.)

If unsportsmanlike conduct occurs, the official may invoke the penalty for the foul or at his discretion may disqualify the player from the game. If two opponents commit fouls simultaneously or on the same play, a double foul is called, for which the replay of point is called.

An error is called whenever (1) the server fails to hit the ball clearly with hand, fist, or arm; (2) the server hits the ball out of bounds, into the net, or fails to hit it completely over the net; (3) a player causes the ball to land out of bounds at any time during play; (4) a player does not clearly hit the ball (the ball may not visibly come to rest at the time it is contacted by the player); (5) one player successively plays the ball (exception: after participating in a multiple block or after having made a simultaneous hit with either a teammate or an opponent, a player may play the ball again); (6) a team plays the ball more than three times before sending it to the opponents' court. (Exception: DGWS— a player participating in a block may not play the ball on the next hit.)

When multiple errors occur, only the first shall be penalized. When fouls and errors occur on the same play, only the foul is penalized.

Several other violations may occur during play. These are summarized as follows: (1) a time-out is charged to a team which fails to substitute without delay; (2) a player entering the game for the fourth time or in the wrong position must leave the game; (3) all points scored are cancelled if made by an improper server or while an illegally entered or positioned re-entry player is on the court; (4) a forfeit game, scoring 15-0, is called if a team does not have six players or refuses to begin play. If after fifteen minutes, the team does not comply with regulations, the match is forfeited. (Exception: DGWS—(1) a team time-out is assessed a team which takes longer than fifteen seconds to complete a substitution; (2) a player making a third entry must leave the game; and (3) no cancellation of points is called for when illegally entered players are on court.)

A *point* is *replayed* whenever (1) an official commits an error; (2) any object enters the court or there is interference with play; (3) a player serves the ball before allowing opponents adequate time to position themselves; (4) a player is injured; (5) a ball simultaneously hit by opponents at the net goes out of bounds; and (6) a double foul occurs.

OFFICIALS

For the purpose of controlling play in a manner equitable to each team, the following officials are used: a referee, an umpire, a timekeeper, a scorekeeper, and two to four linesmen.

The *referee,* the official in charge, is stationed in an elevated position at one end of the net and makes decisions on all playing of the ball, declares point and side-out, and may at anytime overrule another official if he feels an error has occurred.

The *umpire,* stationed at the opposite end of the net from the referee, assists in calling violations regarding positioning, conduct, substitution, and interference with play, as well as making decisions in regard to center line fouls.

The *scorer,* seated near the umpire's position, is charged with keeping an accurate account of the score and all other recorded information, and informing the referee or umpire of violations or fouls committed by either team relative to substitution, positioning, or time-outs.

The *timekeeper* is also near the umpire and scorer and handles all timing devices, accurately recording the actual playing time of the game.

Linesmen are positioned at the rear corners of the court to assist in indicating whether balls are in or out of court. Linesmen also assist in watching to see that a server remains in the serving area and in retrieving the ball when time-outs are called.

DOUBLES RULES

All rules given apply to doubles play except (1) each team's court measures thirty feet by twenty-five feet; (2) no substitutions are permitted; (3) the serve must come from the right half of the service area; (4) a game consists of eleven points or five minutes of actual playing time.

BEACH RULES

All rules given prior to the foregoing section apply except (1) the net is placed seven feet and ten inches above hard packed sand, and seven feet and nine inches above loosely packed sand; (2) teams change courts after each five points scored; (3) ropes are used as boundaries; (4) contact with the center rope is a foul, but if a player's foot is under the rope without contacting it, no foul is called.

INTERNATIONAL RULES

These rules can be briefly differentiated by indicating that (1) players do not call their own fouls; (2) players may not block at the net with more than two men. A blocker may not contact the ball on the first play after the block; (3) the referee starts each serve with a whistle; no noise or shouting is permitted by players; (4) calls are very strict on service reception but become less strict during rallies; and (5) a spiker may follow through over the net if he has touched the ball on his side of the net.

8

Unwritten Laws

Most sports have certain unwritten rules which add flavor to the game. Volleyball is no exception; for example, there is the custom that a player calls his own fouls. During play it is correct, and usually expected, for a player who fouls to indicate the foul and stop play. The calling out of the word "net" indicates (a) that a player touched the net or (b) that the serve touched the net. This habit, acquired by most players, is universally accepted and the person who fails to call his own fouls is soon out of favor. Even during top competition players will raise their hands if they touch a ball going out of bounds or if they have knowingly committed a fault.

Another instance involves the use of open hands while playing the ball below the waist. The rules state that the ball must be distinctly hit. Obviously this can be done with open hands, but in practice the question of the rigidity of the hands has become a sore point. A player who uses the flat open hand(s) to strike the ball will almost invariably be called for "throwing" or "lifting" the ball. The rejection of this type of play may well come from an attempt to overcome bad habits acquired when individuals were permitted to use an underhand toss to guide the ball during play at the grammar school level, and until recently in the girls' rules where a player was permitted to "set up to self," that is, a toss followed by a second hit. At any rate a good practice to follow is to close hands when playing the ball below the waist. This habit will result in cleaner play and will permit the individual to learn the techniques of "bumping" the ball in the forearm bounce pass. This technique is gaining a great deal of popularity and is used almost exclusively in better competition.

A long tradition of good sportsmanship in volleyball has led to an unusual lack of squabbles as a result of a judgment call by an official. Booing and bad conduct in general are rarely witnessed and a quality of friendly rivalry is present at all levels of play. Heckling and other forms of verbal abuse are nonexistent in the game and a person who uses these tactics is soon reminded that such behavior is inappropriate.

Another unwritten law relates to each player's playing in his portion of the court. It is extremely poor form to invade another player's court area to play the ball. "Ball hogs" are one of the crosses beginning players bear. The player who feels he must "help" the other players by taking balls which are out of his area creates many problems and most frequently ruins the game for his fellow players. There are no strict limits for each player but it is asumed that every one has an area of responsibility. It is each team member's responsibility to understand these areas and refrain from taking balls outside his own area unless it is absolutely necessary. This is a particular problem in coeducational play and it is embarrassing when the men must be reminded that the girls "would like to play, too." Volleyball is a team game in the strictest sense and all members of a team want to participate in the competition. Every member is expected to be prepared to assist a teammate in trouble but good sportsmanship requires that each player be permitted to have a try at making the play in that portion of the court in which he is responsible.

Occasionally a player will kick the ball or play it with his foot. There is no rule prohibiting this tactic; therefore it is legal except under DGWS rules. It is used most often when a player is in a position where he cannot reach the ball in time with his hand or forearm. A few players develop great skill at this and are able to set up to a spiker with great accuracy. Kicking is not widely accepted at this time since the emphasis appears to favor diving for the ball.

9

Facts for Enthusiasts

The selection and care of volleyball equipment is relatively simple since there is so little to deal with other than the ball and the net.

The net is a specialized variety three feet wide and thirty-two feet long. It has a black, four-inch square mesh body with double thickness canvas across the top. One-quarter inch manila rope usually is used for suspending the nets, although tournament requirements call for a 7,000 pound, one-fourth inch aircraft cable in the top and and three-sixteenth cable of 2,000 pound test for the bottom in order to insure uniformity. A two-inch vertical tape on the nets marks the court boundary. In addition a three-foot section of three-fourth inch dowel or broomstick is fastened to each end of the net to permit uniform stretch. The net is not permitted to sag more than a quarter-inch in the middle. This usually requires turn-buckle attachments, although the rope is adequate for most play if it is tightened regularly.

The care of a net is a difficult matter since most preservatives have a base which tends to stain the ball. The best advice is to remove the nets and store them indoors when they are not in use and to follow the adage "a stitch in time save nine" when a cord begins to fray.

A volleyball is 25 to 27 inches in circumference with a rubber bladder and leather, laceless cover. The official rules call for a twelve panel ball which weighs between nine and ten ounces, pressurized to seven or eight p.s.i. Adequate pressure adds to ball life. There are other balls on the market including one which has a greater number of panels (to reduce the tendency for imbalance) and many rubber balls. The rubber balls, while adequate for most play, have never been accepted by the better players since there are subtle differences which disturb them. The rubber balls wear well but have the tendency to become slick with use. In cold weather there is also the tendency for rubber to sting when it strikes the arms or hands.

A good leather volleyball may appear to be expensive (about twelve dollars), but its improved playability is well worth this investment. The life of the ball can be lengthened if care is taken to play on smooth surfaces (cement is generally not a smooth surface), and if it is cleaned occasionally with saddle soap.

The costume for volleyball consists of a pair of lightweight gym shoes with good gripping soles and a uniform which permits a great deal of freedom of movement. The latter is particularly important because the bending and stretching maneuvers are quite extreme and improper dress results in restriction, not to mention the problem of ripping.

10

Playing the Game

Volleyball in the United States is played at every conceivable level of skill. The international competition is well regulated by the United States Volleyball Association, which is affiliated with all the organizations within which volleyball is played. The country is divided into fifteen regions which have an internal administration for tournaments.

Within the regions the men and women play in graded competition with AA being the highest. Tournaments are regularly scheduled and teams are drawn from such areas as the Armed Forces, YMCA, athletic clubs, schools, colleges, playgrounds and private enterprises.

Team matches are also scheduled and usually go to the best three of five games. These matches generally do not have any bearing on team standings unless they are scheduled in league play.

Outside the framework of formal competition, one can participate in volleyball at athletic clubs, playgrounds and in schools. It is common practice for one or two nights to be devoted to volleyball in most public or semipublic facilities. Usually the level of play and whether the play is for men's, women's, or mixed groups are designated. Many public facilities schedule adult volleyball which excludes individuals below eighteen for a particular time period.

During the summer months parks and beaches become ideal places to engage in the sport and the level of play improves as the season progresses. The spectator who would like to watch competitive volleyball can write to the United States Volleyball Regional Representative in your area. Addresses and other pertinent information are contained in the Official Guide. This annual rule book and reference guide is published by the USVBA and can be obtained by sending a dollar plus postage to:

U.S.V.B.A. Printer
Box 109
Berne, Indiana

International rules are contained in the 1964 issue and are repeated every four years. In addition, many sporting goods manufacturers publish materials on the rules and equipment.

The enthusiast will also be interested in the *International Volleyball Review,* a journal which can be ordered from Box 554, Encino, California. This publication attempts to keep its subscribers up to date on tournaments, recent developments and problems in volleyball.

A number of volleyball films are also available through All American Productions, 5511 El Cajon Blvd. in San Diego, California.

BIBLIOGRAPHY

1. Division for Girls and Women's Sports. *Volleyball Guide, 1966-68.* Available: American Association for Health, Physical Education, and Recreation, 1201 Sixteenth Street, N.W., Washington, D.C. 20036.

2. Lenoir, Julien, "The World's Championship," *Bulletin Oficiel* (March 1957), pg. 12.

3. Plotnicki, Ben A. "Brief History of Volleyball," University of Tennessee, *70th U.S.V.B.A. Guide, 1965* (U.S.V.B.A., Berne, Indiana), pg. 27-28.

4. Walters, Marshall L. (ed.). *1965 Annual Official Volleyball Rules and Reference Guide of the United States Volleyball Association.* Available: U.S.V.B.A. Printer, Box 109, Berne, Indiana.

5. Welch, J. Edmund, (ed.). "How to Play and Teach Volleyball" (N.Y. Association Press, 1960), pg. 55, 61.